Write On Journaling Templates
Creative Journaling Templates for Classroom & Home

Created & Designed by Dianne J. Hook

ISBN 1-59441-185-9

Contents

Credits

Illustrator: Dianne J. Hook
Project Director: Jennifer Weaver-Spencer
Content Design: Sherrill B. Flora, Jennifer Weaver-Spencer
Cover Production: Annette Hollister-Papp

Introduction to Creative Journal Writing
with the Fun of Decorative Templates

Here are some creative suggestions
for year-round journal writing experiences.

The Purpose of Journals in the Classroom

Journal writing has become increasingly important in today's curriculum. As a teacher, you can make journal writing fun and exciting by providing your students with motivational and creative writing ideas. *Write On Journaling Templates* offers delightful illustrations that will motivate and encourage your young writers.

Journals have many important educational purposes. They can be one of several tools used to evaluate student learning; they can provide regular information about a student's writing; and they can also help students learn to express their thoughts. Journal writing is most effective when used as a regular activity throughout the school week. The length of each session may vary from 10-20 minutes, depending on the age of your students. Provide the students with several copies of journal writing paper. Use the instructions below to create journal paper that changes with the seasons and holidays.

Assembly Instructions for Creating a Journal Page with a Lined Handwriting Template

1. Lined handwriting templates can be found on pages 4-6 of this book. Choose the template that is the most appropriate for the writing abilities of your students. Then, select a decorative border page.

2. Make copies of the lined handwriting template and border of your choice. Cut the lined handwriting template to fit inside the border. Use blue grid paper or a light table to make sure that you have properly centered the writing lines. Attach the template to the inside of the border with doublestick tape or rubber cement.

3. Try to keep a ¼-inch margin on all edges of your paper. If the cutting edges from the lined handwriting template are visible on your first copy, lighten the copy machine setting by one notch. Alternatively, use correction fluid on the first copy, and then use that copy to make the final journal pages for your students.

Instructions for Journaling Templates on CD

Journal pages presented in black and white in this book are available in color on the enclosed CD. If desired, the images can be easily layered to create journal pages. The CD is Mac and PC compatible.

Have fun! Your classroom of students will become eager writers
with the adorable pages from *Write On Journaling Templates.*

Party Bear

7

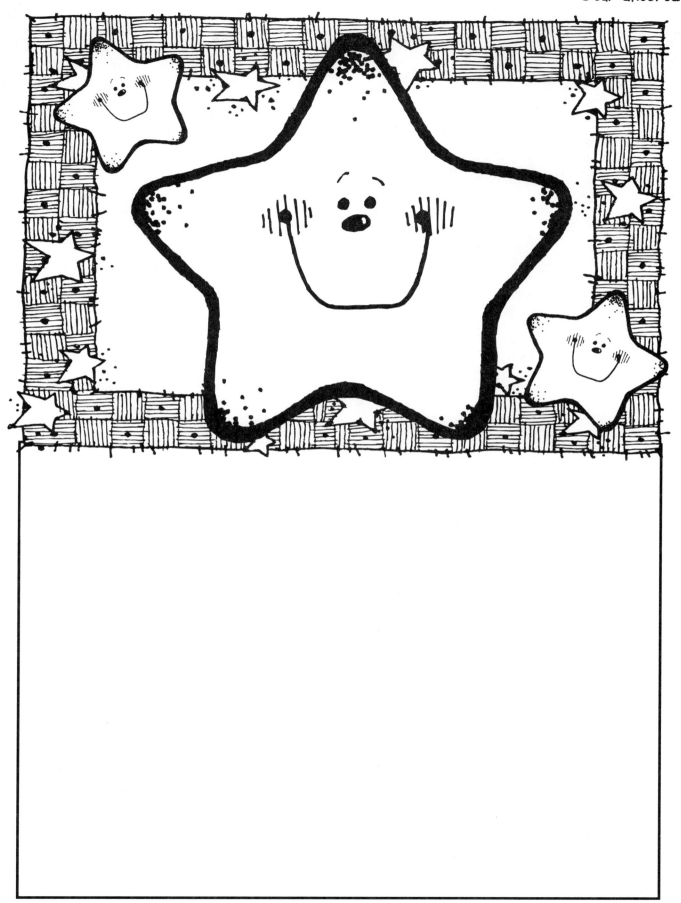

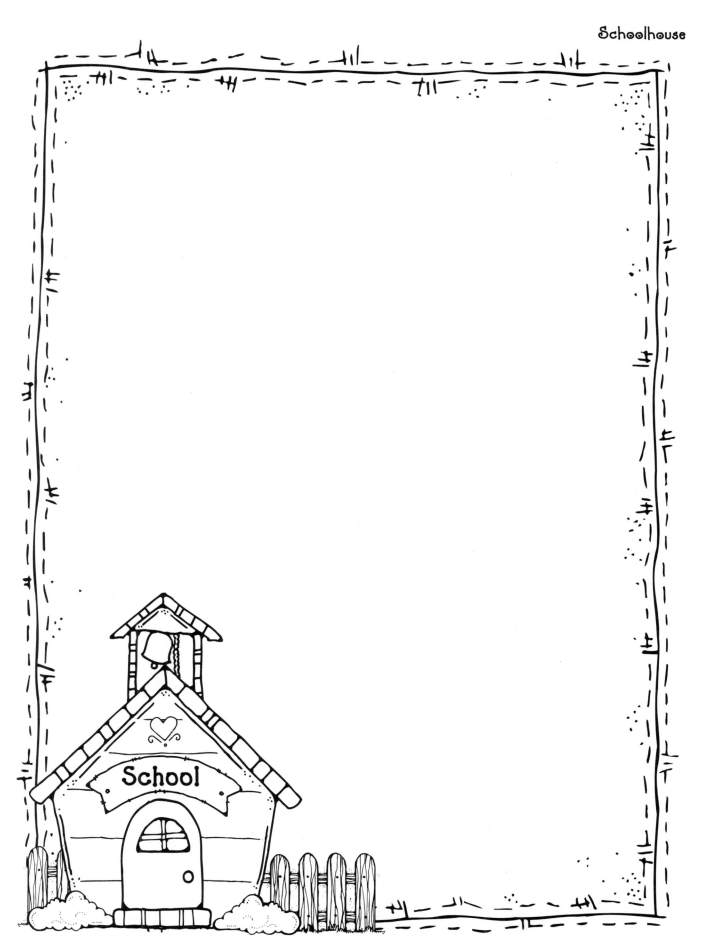

School

Froggie

School Bear

26

Sports

ROUTE

Artist Bear

40

Birthday

49

Alien

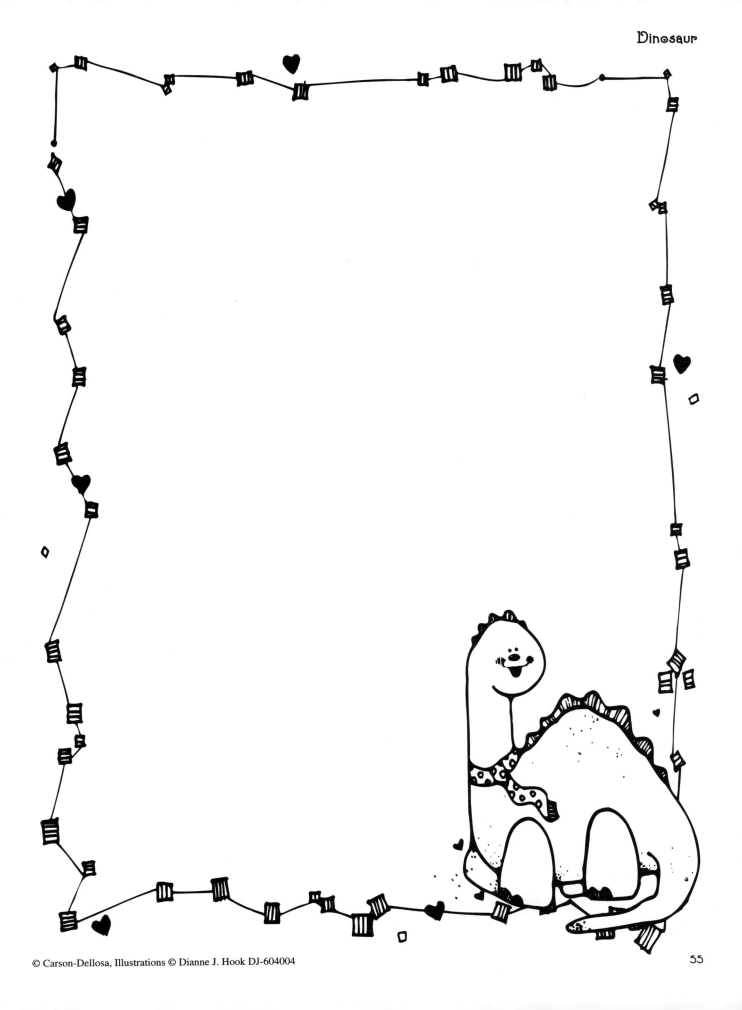

Dinosaur

ALIENBRDR_B

ALIENBRDR2_B

ARTISTBEARBRDR_B

ARTISTBEARBRDR2_B

AWARDBRDR_B

AWARDBRDR2_B

BDAYBRDR_B

BDAYBRDR2_B

BEARSNHEARTSBRDR_B

BOOKBEARBRDR_B

BOOKBEARBRDR2_B

BOOKBEARBRDR3_B

BOOKBEARBRDR4_B

CAMPBEARBRDR_B

CAMPBEARBRDR2_B

COWBOYBEARBRDR_B

COWBOYBEARBRDR2_B

CRAYONBRDR_B

CRAYONBRDR2_B

CRITTERSBRDR_B

CRITTERSBRDR2_B

DINOBRDR_B

DOGGIEMAILBRDR_B

DOGGIEMAILBRDR2_B

FARMBRDR_B

FARMBRDR2_B

FROGGIEBRDR_B

FROGGIEBRDR2_B

HOMEBRDR_B

HOUSEROWBRDR_B

KIDBRDR_B

LETSGOBRDR_B

LETSGOBRDR2_B

PARTYBEARBRDR_B

PARTYBEARBRDR2_B

PETSBRDR_B

PETSBRDR2_B

ROBOTECHBRDR_B

SCHOOLBEARBRDR_B

SCHOOLBEARBRDR2_B

SCHOOLBRDR2_B

SCHOOLSTUFFBRDR_B

SPORTSBRDR_B

SPORTSBRDR2_B

STARBEAR

STARBEAR2_B

STARCHECKBRDR_B

STARCHECKBRDR2_B

STITCHEDBEARBRDR_B

TRIOBEARBRDR_B

TURTLESBRDR2_B

TURTLESBRDR_B

UNDERWATERBRDR_B

WHALEBRDR_B

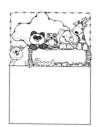
ZOOBRDR_B

ZOOBRDR2_B